WOLVERHAMPTON'S RAILWAYS REVISITED

By Simon Dewey

First Published in 2018 by Simon Dewey
49 Tyninghame Avenue, Tettenhall, Woverhampton WV6 9PP on behalf of the Severn Valley Railway (Wolverhampton Branch)

All distribution enquiries should be addressed to the publisher

Printed by Amadeus Press, Ezra House, West 26 Business Park, Cleckheaton, West Yorkshire BD19 4TQ
Tel (01274) 863210. E-mail: info@amadeuspress.co.uk
Website: www.amadeuspress.co.uk

ISBN 978-0-9565797-1-3

Above: The last working member of the "County" Class 4-6-0's, No 1011 "County of Chester" worked the Wolverhampton to Shrewsbury leg of the Festiniog Railway Society's annual special train from Paddington to Portmadoc on 26th September 1964, having taken over the train from "Clun Castle" at Low Level station during the morning. It returned to Wolverhampton light engine in the afternoon and went onto Oxley shed for servicing where it is seen after coaling ready to go on shed. 1011 was withdrawn 8 weeks later on 21st November and cut up at Cashmore's in Newport in March the following year. *Simon Dewey*

Front Cover: Preserved LNER A3 Pacific "Flying Scotsman" heads away from Wolverhampton station alongside the BCN canal with a special train from Milton Keynes to Shrewsbury on 7th October 1999. The now celebrity locomotive first passed through Wolverhampton on the Festiniog Railway Society's annual special train to Portmadoc in April 1962 running via the Great Western route and Low Level station. *Simon Dewey*

Back Cover: Viewed from Littles Lane bridge is Class 45 No 45 127 which has run forwards out of the High Level station and is about to reverse back into the northern bay platform in August 1985. The cast iron Birmingham Canal Navigations Notice fixed to the bridge warns that "This bridge is insufficient to carry weights beyond the ordinary traffic of the district. By Order". Beyond the railway bridge on which the 45 is standing is Lock Street, which flanked the GWR line northwards out from Low Level station.
45 127 started life as D87 built at Crewe in 1961, lasting until withdrawal in 1987. *Simon Dewey*

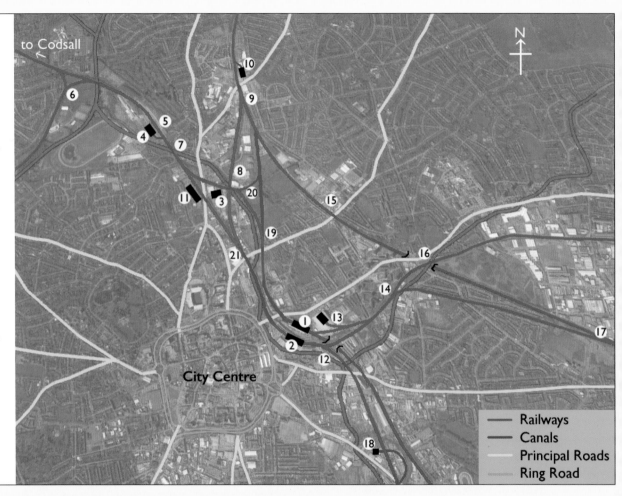

1 Low Level Station

2 High Level Station

3 Stafford Road Shed

4 Oxley Shed

5 Oxley Sidings

6 Oxley Triangle and Wombourn Branch

7 Oxley Viaduct

8 Stour Valley Viaduct

9 Bushbury Junction

10 Bushbury Shed

11 Stafford Road Junction and Stafford Road Works

12 Crane Street Junction

13 Wednesfield Road Goods Depot

14 Heath Town Junction

15 Grand Junction Line ("The Old Line")

16 Heath Town Tunnel

17 Portobello Junction

18 Wolverhampton Steel Terminal

19 Cannock Road Junction

20 Bushbury Chord

21 Wolverhampton North Junction

to Codsall

City Centre

Railways
Canals
Principal Roads
Ring Road

Introduction

This book is a companion to "Wolverhampton's Railways in Colour" published in 2010. The geographical scope of both books, being limited to Wolverhampton's boundaries (although extending a couple of miles beyond on the line towards Shrewsbury) is the same but the intention has been to supplement the images contained in the earlier book and update them to some extent.

While not in the First Division of railway towns such as Swindon and Crewe, Wolverhampton was certainly an important member of the Second, its Stafford Road Works of the GWR for some time rivalling Swindon for importance with approaching one thousand locomotives being built here as well as numerous rebuilds, between the 1850's and early 1900's .

The city's railway history is quite complex and includes two notorious "railway battles" fought by rival companies during the relative dawn of the railway age in 1850 and 1851 respectively but this book covers predominantly the latter days of steam and early days of the "modern" era, picturing the railways through the town as they were and are some 110 to 150 years later.

The railway landscape changed dramatically during the 1960's with the legacy of the GWR, once the major player in Wolverhampton's railway activities, being all-but eradicated. Gone are its locomotive works, engine sheds and goods depots but its principal station, the Low Level, remains, albeit not in railway or any associated use and shorn of its Up side buildings and platforms. A plan to convert the station to a transport heritage centre celebrating Wolverhampton's industrial and transport manufacturing history, initiated in the mid 1980's, sadly came to nought and despite the city's almost unrivalled past as a centre for building most forms of vehicles which either ran on wheels or flew in the air such an establishment remains yet to be achieved.

The railway as it now remains is centred on the ex LMS routes through what is now the city with all but the line towards Shrewsbury north of Oxley electrified.

The book starts at the Low Level station, then visits the engine sheds at Stafford Road and Oxley before following the GWR route towards Shrewsbury as far as Codsall, returning to Wolverhampton proper to cover the various lines and establishments including Bushbury shed, Stafford Road Works, the High Level station and the more important goods depots, as well as the route of the Grand Junction Railway, the then town's first railway of the 1830's, known locally as "The Old Line".

Reference to the accompanying map should assist in identifying the various locations for those not familiar with the area.

A few of the photographs included are unfortunately not of the finest quality but are included for their historic value or interest.

As with previous books, the High Level lines in steam days seem to have received relatively scant coverage in colour photographs compared with the Low Level and GWR route and this is reflected in the book. As one contributor put it " A platform ticket for the Low Level bought you much better value than one for the High Level …"

Sadly, since publication of the earlier book several of the photographers whose work has been included in either or both of the books have died and this book is dedicated to the memory of particularly Brian Robbins, John Bucknall and Hugh Ballantyne, all excellent railway photographers.

Thanks are due to the following (in no particular order) who have made their photographs available or provided assistance much appreciated by the author:-

Doug Nicholson, Ned Williams, Alan Davies, David Rostance, Richard Icke, Lawrence Brownhill, Paul Dorney, Mike Page, Roger Fletcher, Bob Yate, Mervyn Srodzinsky, Colin Moss, Peter Share, Dave Rowley, Eric Bickley and my wife Christine. Also the late John Hendley's estate.

Simon Dewey, Tettenhall, Wolverhampton, 2018

Low Level Station

This was the GWR's principal station in Wolverhampton, opened in 1854 and operating as such until 1967 and in reduced roles until 1972. It was a staging post for long distance trains passing through the town with locomotives being changed there.

From June to September 1965 three "Britannia" Pacifics were transferred from Holyhead to Oxley to work Summer season South coast and West of England "extras" – Nos 70045 "Lord Rowallan", unnamed 70047 and 70053 "Moray Firth".

70045, stripped of its nameplates but wearing a neatly stencilled 2B shedcode has ash brushed off its running plate by its driver before setting off with the 10.00 train to Kingswear on 10th July 1965.

After its stay at Oxley the locomotive went to Banbury for three months before being transferred North to Carlisle in January 1966 from where it was withdrawn in December 1967.

Mike Page

A southbound express has arrived at the main Up platform also on 24th July 1965 behind Stanier Black 5 4-6-0 No 45434 which will leave the train to be replaced by Oxley shed's "Grange" class No 6870 "Bodicote Grange" standing on the adjacent middle road. The ex LMS engine will then reverse back through the station and on towards Oxley shed for servicing. While 6870 still carries its smokebox numberplate it has lost its nameplates and cabside numberplates and its grimy appearance (as with that of the Black 5) betokens the rapidly advancing run-down of steam locomotives, with the "Grange" destined for withdrawal only two months later, in September 1965.

The lofty brick wall extending almost the full length of the station once supported an all-over roof which was removed in the 1930's, cover to the affected platforms being replaced by the canopies visible. The structure in the right background was the carriage shed at the rear of the station. *Paul Dorney*

Looking South from the main Down platform on 25th June 1965 Class 47 No D1733 is seen waiting on one of the middle roads to take on the 13.35 Wolverhampton to Paddington train which will follow the relief train that has arrived at the adjacent platform 3 behind Black 5 No 44812, after it departs South.

D1733 had the honour of being the prototype locomotive for the new XP64 blue livery devised by British Railways in their moves to develop their corporate image in 1964, when it also carried the first example of the now iconic double arrow logo, applied in white on red panels below the cabside windows.

Wolverhampton South signalbox stands adjacent to 44812 with Sun Street bridge beyond, through the arch of which can be seen the two Northern portals of Wolverhampton tunnel through which the steam train will soon pass.   *Mike Page*

"Modified Hall" 4-6-0 No 7929 "Wyke Hall " but devoid of its nameplates and cabside numberplates stands at the Southern end of the main Up platform ready to depart with a Barmouth to Birmingham Summer Saturday extra on 24th July 1965 which 7929 had brought forwards from Shrewsbury.

Nothing in the photograph now remains, even Sun Street bridge having disappeared and the road realigned when the land beyond it was redeveloped to form a Post Office sorting and distribution centre.

7929 was the last of the class to be built, in November 1950 and withdrawn in August 1965 with a recorded mileage during its 15-year working life of 512,080 miles"   *Paul Dorney*

"King" class No 6026 "King John" enters the main Down platform from below Sun Street bridge in about 1961 with an express from Paddington.

From the early 1930's until the onset of the 1962 Winter timetable "Kings" had been the mainstay of motive power on the Wolverhampton- Birmingham – Paddington expresses with Stafford Road shed maintaining an allocation of members of the class from 1928, when 6017 "King Edward IV" was delivered new from Swindon.

From the author's point of view, certainly in the latter days of their existence "King John" was possibly the least frequent visitor of the class to Wolverhampton, although it had been shedded here between March 1935 and October 1939. It was withdrawn in June 1962 from Old Oak Common with an accumulated mileage of 1,622,350 miles.

The house visible in the background above the locomotive's tender was the Low Level Stationmaster's house.

John Hendley Collection

In September 1962 the "Pines Express" from Manchester to Bournemouth was rerouted to use Western Region lines through Wolverhampton and the ex-GWR route from Birmingham Snow Hill to Oxford and Reading to join the Southern Region Waterloo to Bournemouth line at Basingstoke. This brought frequent appearances of LMR Class 40 Diesels as well as "Royal Scots" to the Low Level where locomotives were usually changed.

Class 40 No D254 is seen entering Low Level on the southbound working in snowy weather in early 1964. The Diesel's steam heating boiler is obviously working and its effects in the train no doubt much appreciated.

Alan Davies Collection

One Saturday in late July or early August 1964 "Royal Scot" No 46160 "Queen Victoria's Rifleman" waits in the Shrewsbury Bay platform at the Northern end of the station ready to take forward train 1M02, the Saturday duplicate "Pines Express" 09.23 Bournemouth to Liverpool train, which will leave at about 14.30 travelling via Shrewsbury and Crewe.

In preparation for use of Low Level as a parcels concentration depot between 1970 and 1981 the bay was infilled but during sadly abortive works to convert the station to a museum celebrating Wolverhampton's history as a major transport manufacturing centre the infilling was removed. The work to remove the infilling revealed the remains of a length of Mixed Gauge track however, which has fortunately been retained in situ and protected within a brick-walled pit within the floor of the banqueting suite now occupying the Down side part of the station building retained.

46160 was built in August 1930 at the Derby works of the LMS, rebuilt with a taper boiler in 1945 and withdrawn 20 years later in May 1965.   *Lawrence Brownhill*

Pioneer "King" No 6000 "King George V" attracts much youthful attention at the North end of the main Down platform in about 1961 having arrived from Paddington with the "Cambrian Coast Express" which it will take forward to Shrewsbury.

Prominent on the front footplate is the bell presented by the Baltimore & Ohio Railway as a memento of 6000's visit to the USA in 1927 to take part in their centenary celebrations, together with the two medallions above the cabside numberplate. *John Hendley Collection*

The GWR Engine Sheds

The GWR in Wolverhampton had two engine sheds, at Stafford Road and Oxley. The former was the older, being established in 1854 (as a Broad Gauge shed) but as the importance of Wolverhampton grew and traffic expanded further locomotive accommodation was necessary and Oxley was built, opening in 1907, housing principally freight and shunting locomotives.

Stafford Road

A view across Stafford Road shed yard in about 1959 with the shed's steam breakdown crane in action on an unidentified task on the right. "Castle" No 5073 "Blenheim" stands on the left with a "Hall" behind it while another "Castle" and a "Hall" occupy the line beyond the crane.

The shed was coded SRD by the GWR, changing in 1948, on Nationalisation of the railways, to 84A.

The building in the extreme background is the 1930's-built repair shop of Stafford Road Works, in front of which is the roof of the 1870's – built Lower Yard Erecting Shop of an earlier manifestation of the Works. To the left is the front of the straight road shed which normally housed the larger locos of 84A's allocation. This building started life in 1854 as a Broad Gauge engine shed, subsequently being extended forwards and used as the Tender and Paint Shops of the 1870's configuration of the Works before reverting to use as an engine shed, this time for Standard Gauge locomotives.

Lawrence Brownhill

The straight road shed forms the background to another late 1950's view in the shed yard with "King" class 4-6-0 No 6028 "King George VI" simmering gently in the foreground with a wisp of steam from its safety valve, ready for its next turn of duty southwards. 6028 was never a Wolverhampton-based engine having been shedded variously during its life at Old Oak Common, Newton Abbott and Cardiff Canton. It was one of the last of the class to be withdrawn, unlike Stafford Road's 6006 "King George I" which was the first, in February 1962.

Another "King" also in sparkling condition can be seen in the background beyond the 84XX pannier tank in what was sadly the more usual state of cleanliness of the shed's locomotives towards the end of the shed's life.

F G Richardson/Ned Williams Collection

While freight, tank and mixed traffic locomotives constituted the bulk of the types entering Stafford Road Works for repair during the twentieth century, visits by express classes such as "Castles" and even "Kings" were not unknown, although usually for Light Casual or Unclassified attention only.

The last "Castle" to visit the works was No 5071 "Spitfire" in 1963 for Light Casual repair, entering on 5th April and leaving on 8th May. It is seen in the yard of Stafford Road shed after its repair before being returned to its home shed of Bristol St Philip's Marsh, the extent of any repainting being only its smokebox and chimney. It would have little more than five months further use, however, being withdrawn on 22nd October 1963 with an accumulated mileage during its life of 1,150,913 miles.

Simon Dewey

The GWR "Kings" were arguably the most prestigious locomotives based at Wolverhampton in the mid-20th Century and Stafford Road in its penultimate year of operation, 1962, boasted being home to no fewer than 15 of the class variously during that year, although some were transferred away.

An unidentified Stafford Road "King" is seen reversing towards the bridge over the canal towards the shed yard having been turned, watered and coaled at the coaling stage following arrival at Wolverhampton Low Level with a train from Paddington in about 1961. After crossing the canal locomotives would pass beneath the Stour Valley line viaduct seen in the background to reach the shed yard, the coaling stage lying remote from it on the Eastern side of the canal and the shed on the Western side. *Lawrence Brownhill*

Parked adjacent to the Eastern side of the coaling stage at Stafford Road on 22nd June 1963 is 9F 2-10-0 No 92154 then allocated to Wellingborough. The purpose of its appearance in Wolverhampton is unknown although possibly connected with the arrival of at least one pigeon fanciers' special train which had brought Stanier Pacific 46256 "Sir William Stanier FRS" also to Stafford Road that day. It would shortly be passed by LNWR "Super D" 0-8-0 No 49361 heading back from visiting Oxley as part of an SLS tour of lines in the West Midlands.

The running lines curving round to Stafford Road Junction lie beyond the 9F, beyond which are lines used for carriage storage.
Freight engines, other than locally-based tank engines, were not frequently seen on Stafford Road shed other than in connection with their occasional use on passenger trains. Stafford Road shed closed in September 1963, its locomotive allocation being transferred to Oxley or withdrawn.
Doug Nicholson

GWR "King" Class No 6015 "King Richard III" taking water after turning and before coaling at the coal stage at Stafford Road shed in about 1959. The engine had arrived in Wolverhampton with "The Inter City" named train, having left Paddington at 9a.m., reaching the Low Level station about 2½ hours later and will return Southwards in the afternoon, departing from Low Level at 4.35p.m. reaching London at 7.10pm.

As well as the train reporting number of the time, the loco carries on its smokebox door the later, more elaborate and colourful headboard which featured the coats of arms of London, Birmingham and Wolverhampton.

6015, built in June 1928 accumulated 1,901,585 miles in its life, being withdrawn in September 1962 from Stafford Road, having been transferred there from Old Oak Common 3 months earlier. It was cut up at Cox & Danks in Oldbury during April 1963.

The turntable pit is visible in the foreground and although stripped of the turntable itself and all associated mechanism, at the time of writing still remains to be seen just off the nearby canal towpath.

F G Richardson / Ned Williams Collection

Saltley-based Stanier 8F No 48351 shunts a single coal wagon at Oxley shed on 15th November 1966.

The shed's coaling stage occupies the centre of the photograph with to its left, the ash pit area. The tracks leading up to the coaling stage gave access to the interior of the structure for trucks of locomotive coal from which the coal was transferred to large tubs manhandled

out onto tilting platforms to tip up and discharge into the tenders or bunkers of waiting locomotives. Locomotives could be coaled from either side of the structure but the Western side (that to the left) was the most used.

48351 was transferred following the closure of Saltley shed also in March 1967 to Trafford Park, Manchester from where it was withdrawn in January 1968. *David Rostance*

Well off its beaten track is Southern Region rebuilt "Merchant Navy" Class Pacific No 35027 "Port Line" seen leaving Oxley shed after servicing to return South on 12th March 1966, having worked a football special from Southampton for the Wolves v Southampton match on that day.

Visits of Bulleid Pacifics to Wolverhampton were not unknown during the 1960's, usually on Society or football specials, with instances being recorded at both Stafford Road and Oxley sheds.

35022 was built at Eastleigh in December 1948 and rebuilt from its airsmoothed casing condition to its later more conventional appearance in May 1957. Following withdrawal in September 1966 it was sold to Woodham Brothers for scrap, lying in their scrapyard at Barry for 16 years until being rescued for preservation by the Swindon & Cricklade Railway, subsequently moving to the Bluebell Railway where it was restored and returned to steam in 1988. It is currently undergoing further restoration at the East Lancs Railway.

Brian Robbins

18

Oxley shed as seen on 4th February 1967, a month before closure with Stanier Black 5 No 44685, Crosti-boilered BR 9F 2-10-0 no 92027 and Stanier 8F No 48402 visible. Although originally a GWR shed, by this time all ex GWR locomotives had gone and the shed's steam allocation was of ex LMS and BR types. As well as the Diesel shunters which were based there for working Oxley Sidings, the shed also played host to a variety of main line Diesel locomotives, particularly Brush Sulzer Type 4's (TOPS class 47). These had replaced the Class 52 "Westerns" which commenced Diesel haulage of the Paddington expresses at the onset of the 1962 Winter timetable, when the "Kings" were withdrawn.

The three gables forming the Southern frontage of the shed building are, from left to right, the lifting/repair shop, the main entrance to the cavernous interior of the shed itself and the offices and stores respectively.

The shed closed on March 5th 1967 but remained in use for carrying out minor repairs and servicing of steam locomotives visiting specifically for the purpose for a few months. It closed officially on 1st January 1968 and was almosttotally demolished during the summer of that year with the site subsequently being redeveloped as a train servicing depot, most recently for Virgin "Pendolino" units.

David Rostance

Until its final years Oxley was almost exclusively a freight, mixed traffic and shunting locomotive shed, stabling and servicing a wide variety of such engines.

Upper photo: BR's final design of freight locomotives were the 9F 2-10-0's and No 92220 "Evening Star" was the very last steam locomotive built by British Railways, entering traffic in March 1960. Its active life was very short, the locomotive being withdrawn almost precisely 5 years later in March 1965.
It is seen at Oxley in the summer of 1963 in the company of 0-6-0 pannier tanks on one of the lines near the coaling stage during its short career, having brought in a freight train to Oxley Sidings from the South. *Doug Nicholson*

Lower photo: From an older generation, GWR 28xx class 2-8-0 No 2839 of Newport Ebbw Junction shed, its tender piled high with coal and long-handled fire irons leaning against the cab, stands also in the shed yard in 1963. Oxley maintained a stud of these locomotives for many years although by the early 1960's only later examples with side window cabs were shedded there.
2839 was built at Swindon in 1912 and lasted until 1964, exceeding the length of 92220's working life by almost half a century. *Simon Dewey*

On the closure of Stafford Road shed in September 1963 most of its remaining allocation of locomotives was transferred to Oxley, the most important being nine of its ten "Castles", Oxley hitherto having been a freight locomotive shed. The tenth engine, 7001 "Sir James Milne" was withdrawn when Stafford Road closed.

In January 1963 control of the Western Region's Wolverhampton District passed to the London Midland Region and Oxley shed, previously coded 84B was recoded 2B.

"Castle" No 5063 "Earl Baldwin", one of the engines transferred from Stafford Road and wearing its 2B shedplate, is seen in July 1964 alongside the Western side of the shed together with No 7023 "Penrice Castle" (transferred to Oxley the previous month) which is standing in the side doorway which gave access to the Northern turntable within the shed itself. Both engines are in clean condition with 5063 having been prepared to tow the royal train carrying the Queen Mother back from Stratford-on-Avon to Windsor on 12th July 1964. Their cleanliness sadly would not last, the latter-day Oxley livery being distinctly grimy.

Oxley's "Castles" survived until the latter part of 1964 much used on Summer Saturday holiday expresses to the West Country via Stratford-on-Avon and the South Coast via Oxford and on Christmas parcels trains that year. 7023 was the last one in steam, dropping its fire for the last time on 24th January 1965 with official withdrawal, together with that of her sister engines taking place the following month. *Eric Hamilton/Ned Williams Collection*

Moguls

BR Standard Class 2 2-6-0 No 78008 in about July 1963 at the Northern end of the Western side of the shed. Built at Darlington in 1953, the engine was allocated to the Western Region for the whole of its life, ending up at Oxley following the closure of Stafford Road in 1963 to which it had been transferred from Worcester the previous year. In its unlined green livery it was used on relatively light workings in the Wolverhampton area including hauling the local District Engineer's inspection saloon, being withdrawn in October 1966 and scrapped the following January.

The large doorway visible behind the locomotive was incorporated into the shed when built but was never used, being intended to provide access to a third turntable within the building should it be enlarged, which never occurred. *Doug Nicholson*

GWR Chuchward 43XX No 5369, a Tyseley engine at the time, at the end of a line of parked locomotives also alongside the shed building in mid-summer 1963. It represents a successful and useful class of locomotives of which Oxley maintained a significant number during their lives. Introduced in 1911 and totalling 341 examples, almost a third of the total were allocated to the sheds of the Wolverhampton Division with 13 being allocated to Oxley in the probably typical year of 1957.

5369 was built at Swindon in May 1919, being renumbered 8369 in 1928 when it and others of the class were modified to alter their weight distribution, reverting to its original form and number in 1944. It was withdrawn only months after the photograph was taken, in November 1963. *Doug Nicholson*

The shed's allocation during its final year or so was exclusively of ex LMS and BR Standard locomotives. In the scene typical of inside the shed in the run-up towards closure only 3 weeks after the photograph was taken on 11th February 1967 LMS Black 5 4-6-0 No 44856 stands cold on one of the lines radiating from the Southern turntable, the pit of which dominates the foreground, its wooden deck covering having been removed a few years before. On the left, Stanier 8F 2-8-0 No 48407, also parked, is in steam and still active. On the shed's closure on 5th March the 8F was transferred initially to Stoke-on-Trent and subsequently to Heaton Mersey from where it was withdrawn in December 1967.

It is doubtful if 44856 ever worked again being officially withdrawn on 18th February 1967.

David Rostance

Another view inside the shed but about a year earlier, with BR Standard Class 5 4-6-0 No 73019, an Oxley-shedded engine at the time, stored out of use off the rearward (Northern) turntable with its timber deck covering retained in place seen behind the locomotive. Despite steam locomotive withdrawals proceeding at a rapid pace by then and 73019's rusty wheels testifying to its clearly not having run for some time, its active days were not over since it was transferred in April 1966 to Bolton from where it was not withdrawn until January 1967.

Among the locomotives visible in the background is a then still relatively new Class 47 Diesel in its two-tone green livery, one of a batch (Nos D1691 to D1698) transferred from the Western Region and notionally allocated to Oxley in January 1966. With the London Midland Region acquiring control of the ex Western Region lines north of Birmingham in 1963 and their dislike of Diesel Hydraulics, these Diesel electrics replaced the Class 52 "Western" Diesel hydraulics which had ousted steam haulage of the Paddington-Wolverhampton-Chester principal expresses in 1962. *Brian Robbins*

Parked by the Eastern side of the shed in about March 1965 are seen two LMS "Jubilee" 4-6-0's, withdrawn and on their way to Cashmore's at Great Bridge for scrapping, No 45595 "Southern Rhodesia" and an unidentified member of the class behind. Oxley Sidings and the shed complex saw a wide variety of "foreign" locomotives on their way to the Midlands for scrapping during the mid-1960's as BR dispensed with its steam locomotive fleet, including LMS "Duchesses" and at least one LNER A1 Pacific being recorded.

The heavily smoke-stained Eastern doorway giving access into the shed is prominent next to the building housing the shed's stationary boilers and sand hearth where sand for use in locomotives' sand boxes was dried.

Brian Robbins

(Below) Another "Jubilee" No 45577 "Bengal", still active, stands alongside the sandstone escarpment from which the upper photograph was taken, in 1963. It would last only one year more before being withdrawn in September 1964.

Doug Nicholson

Bushbury shed's remaining small complement of locomotives was transferred away mainly to Bescot, when the shed closed on 12th April 1965 but with four ending up at Oxley - LMS Stanier 2-cylinder 2-6-4T No 42604 together with three Stanier Moguls. While the Moguls were kept busy at their new base, the large tank engine, despite receiving a neatly stencilled 2B shedcode on the smokebox door, was destined to see little further use, being condemned only weeks later on 8th May. The locomotive is seen two months later standing abandoned at the rear of the shed amongst rose bay willow herb prior to eventually being towed away and scrapped during September 1965.

Doug Nicholson

Oxley Sidings, lying immediately to the North of Oxley Viaduct and extending both sides of the line to Shrewsbury were one of the GWR's major marshalling yards with over 40 lines of sidings and loops, the longest capable of accommodating trains of up to 70 wagons.

Seen at Oxley Sidings on 22nd June 1963 was LNWR "Super D" 0-8-0 No 49361 visiting on an SLS special train touring West Midland lines behind one of the last of the ex LNWR locomotives. In this photograph the locomotive is running round its train, having run tender-first from Dudley and will return forwards to couple up to its train ready to depart South via the Low Level station and up the spur linking this and the previous Midland Railway line from High Level to Walsall at Heath Town Junction to continue its trip.

The running lines of the Shrewsbury route through the sidings lie to the Right of the "Super D" with beyond them the elevated lines of the Up side sidings. *Richard Icke*

Another special train passing through Wolverhampton and halting at Oxley Sidings while its passengers visited the shed was a Derbyshire Locomotive Society train from Leeds to Crewe on 24th March 1963. Hauled throughout by "Clan" Pacific No 72008 "Clan MacCleod" it was piloted from Tyseley by Modified Hall No 7929 "Wyke Hall".

The pair are seen in Oxley Sidings awaiting return of their passengers before continuing North." *Alan Davies Collection*

On the same day as the visit of the Super D on 22nd June 1963, GWR "Hall" class 4-6-0 No 6906 "Chicheley Hall" backs down onto its train of sheeted-over wagons and Toad brake van prior to leaving Southwards , preceding the "Super D" and its special train towards Wolverhampton. Along with the "Grange" class 4-6-0's, the "Halls" and their modified sisters arguably provided the mainstay of the GWR's mixed traffic locomotive fleet from their introduction in 1928. Both Oxley and Stafford Road sheds maintained allocations of "Halls" and "Modified Halls" throughout the life of the class.

"Chicheley Hall" was built at Swindon in November 1940 and was almost 25 years old when condemned , following being stopped with wasted boiler tubes, on 3rd April 1965 having run 752,116 miles during its life.

Alan Davies Collection

In more recent times, seen leaving the Northern end of Oxley Sidings is Class 60 No 60 078 with a Merry-Go-Round train of loaded coal hoppers for Ironbridge Power Station in September 1992. The carriage-washing plant of Oxley train servicing depot occupies the line behind the locomotive. Workings to Ironbridge Power Station ceased when it closed in November 2015 since when freight workings along the Wolverhampton to Shrewsbury line have been neglible. The Class 60's, 3100hp Diesel electric Co-Co locomotives, were introduced between 1989 and 1991 and were effectively the swan song of British built main line locomotives, subsequent types being of American or Continental origin.

Simon Dewey

In sadly not the best of photographs rebuilt "Royal Scot" 4-6-0 No 46110 "Grenadier Guardsman" heads away from Wolverhampton with the Northbound "Pines Express" to Manchester from Bournemouth in the summer of 1963. The two lines occupying the foreground are those sweeping round to the Wombourn (the GWR never spelled it Wombourne) Branch

Prior to the previous year the train had used LMS metals, usually passing through Wolverhampton on the Grand Junction line ("The Old Line") to Bescot, then Walsall, where locomotives were changed, thence round the Sutton Park line to Birmingham and on via the

MR route to Bath. From Bath the train travelled along the Somerset & Dorset route to Poole and Bournemouth West. In September 1962 the "Pines" was re-routed via Wolverhampton Low Level, Oxford, Basingstoke and Southampton. Locomotives were now changed at Wolverhampton with usually a Stafford Road "Castle" on the leg to and from Oxford where they were again changed, this time to a Southern Region locomotive.

46110 was built in 1927 by the North British Locomotive Company to the original Fowler design and rebuilt to Stanier's larger, taper-boilered design with double chimney and new cylinders in 1953. It was withdrawn in February 1964.   *Simon Dewey*

A little further North from the previous two photographs the lines cross the Staffs & Worcester canal, the truncated remains of the Wombourn Branch continuing in the foreground to buffers just beyond one of the pair of bridges over the waterway (where a coal train to Ironbridge came to grief in April 1985 - see page 51 in "Wolverhampton's Railways in Colour").

Through services to Shrewsbury from London continued after cessation of other than limited local services via Low Level in March 1967 but from Euston following electrification of the LMS route, with trains changing from electric to Diesel haulage at High Level station and vice versa. The introduction of Driving Van Trailers (DVT's) in 1988 obviated the need for locomotives to be changed at Euston following the Southbound journey, the trains being capable of being driven from the DVT marshalled at the South end of the train with the electric locomotive retained at the North. Beyond Wolverhampton however the ex GWR line remained (and still does) unelectrified and Diesel locomotives had to be substituted for the rest of the journey. The DVT remained in position at the end of the train but unlike the electric loco the Diesel always had to lead the train.

(Above) A Southbound working from Shrewsbury to Euston is seen approaching Oxley in 1992 not long before these through services were terminated, with a Class 47 leading the DVT and the whole train in the then Intercity Executive livery.

(Left) Diesel multiple units commenced running Western Region local services through Wolverhampton Low Level in June 1957, BR Derby high density 3-car units (which became Class 116) being used. A Class 116 unit in BR blue and grey livery with a West Midlands PTE WM logo on its front crosses the same bridge over the Staffs & Worcester canal as in the picture above on a Shrewsbury to Wolverhampton train in June 1986.   *Both : Simon Dewey*

The Wombourn Branch formation after crossing the canal occupies the middle distance in the right of the photograph as LMS 8F No 48073, unusually working its train tender-first, heads away from Oxley in semi rural settings along the main line to Shrewsbury with a Down goods train on 19ᵗʰ January 1967.

Built in 1936 at Vulcan Foundry, Newton-le-Willows 48073 was at the time of the photograph based at Saltley. On closure of that shed to steam in March 1967 it was transferred to Chester where it spent less than a month before being withdrawn and sent to Cashmore's at Great Bridge for scrapping.

David Rostance

Southern Region Unrebuilt "Battle of Britain" Pacific No 34064 "Fighter Command" is seen crossing Oxley Moor Road a little beyond the location of the previous photograph on 28th September 1963, running about 45 minutes late working that year's Talyllyn R.P.S special train from Paddington to Towyn as far as Ruabon.

While rebuilt Bulleid Pacifics were not unknown visitors to Wolverhampton, unrebuilt examples were distinct rarities. Built at Brighton in 1947 and withdrawn in May 1966 34064 was unique within the class by being fitted with a Giesl ejector in 1962.

Doug Nicholson

The triangle of lines formed between Oxley Middle, Branch and North Junctions was not infrequently used to turn locomotives such as when the turntable at Stafford Road was out of use or too busy. The main Shrewsbury line forming the Northern leg of the triangle occupies the background as smartly turned out Ivatt Class 2 2-6-0 No 46429 of Bescot shed passes round the Eastern leg between Oxley Middle and Branch Junctions with the District Engineer's inspection saloon in July 1963. It will then reverse the saloon round the third leg from Branch to North Junction before again reversing direction to head locomotive-first back along the main line towards Wolverhampton.

46429 was built at Crewe in 1948, lasting in traffic until July 1966 and scrapped during that October.

Simon Dewey

A different view of newly-built Class 52 Diesel hydraulic No D1047 "Western Lord" at the head of the freight train it had brought from Crewe in February 1963, seen here from the accommodation bridge off Aldersley Road, visible in the background.

The 52 was working its way on delivery to the Western Region from Crewe Works. Having brought the train round onto the Branch from Oxley North Junction, it will uncouple, run forwards to Branch Junction then reverse to run light engine round the eastern leg of the triangle to Oxley shed. The train itself, probably the 11.00 a.m. Crewe to Bristol, will continue its journey along the Branch but behind a replacement steam locomotive which will have come round from Oxley to take it forward.

Doug Nicholson

Codsall

About 3 miles North of the Oxley triangle is Codsall with its station dating from the opening of the Shrewsbury & Birmingham Railway in 1849.

Views from the station footbridge looking South and North respectively with *(above)* a 2-car Metro Cammell Class 101 DMU in distinctive Strathclyde livery, having been transferred from Glasgow to Tyseley but not repainted, calls at the station in September 1991 forming a stopping train to Shrewsbury. No fewer than 760 vehicles forming Class 101 were delivered between 1956 and 1960 variously to all but the Southern Region. They worked their last passenger duties in 2003. The Down side station building is now a pub.

(Right) Class 58 heavy freight Co-Co No 58 002 is seen heading in the Wolverhampton direction with empty MGR coal hoppers from Ironbridge power station in September 1992. Loaded workings North and their empty Southbound returns ceased upon closure of the power station in 2015 and at the time of writing freight traffic along the line is very sparse. *Both: Simon Dewey*

Oxley South and Viaduct

Network SouthEast-liveried Class 47 No 47 573 runs light engine towards Oxley viaduct and the Oxley signal box opened to replace the various Oxley and Stafford Road Junction boxes in 1968. This box itself was decommissioned in November 2010.

The tracks in the foreground formed the access to Oxley shed and latterly to the Alstom Train Care Depot that was built on its site after demolition.

NSE was one of three passenger sectors of British Rail formed in 1982 principally operating commuter trains in the London area and inter-urban services in the Southeast. It was disbanded in 1994. Both Diesel and electric locomotives in NSE livery could be seen from time to time in Wolverhampton.

Simon Dewey

Oxley viaduct seen from Jones Road, Dunstall on 17th June 2006 as Virgin Class 57 No 57 311 "Parker" drags a Virgin Pendolino unit away from Oxley sidings where it will have been serviced, up to Wolverhampton station to form an express to Euston. The electric overhead power supply was temporarily turned off due to engineering works south of Birmingham necessitating the Pendolino being Diesel-dragged as far as Nuneaton to join the West Coast main line before being able to proceed under its own power southwards . The skew arch of the viaduct below the leading coach of the Pendolino spans the BCN canal on its way down the 21 locks between Broad Street basin near the centre of Wolverhampton and Aldersley Junction where it joins the Staffs & Worcester canal.

The Class 57's were created from Class 47's with new engines and control systems, those operated by Virgin Trains and intended for rescue duties being named after characters from the "Thunderbirds" TV series.

Simon Dewey

Oxley viaduct seen through one of the arches of the Stour Valley viaduct across the Smestow valley with a Class 31 Brush A1A-A1A locomotive heading out of Oxley carriage sidings with the empty stock of a Birmingham to Norwich train in August 1983. Both structures are of blue brick, Oxley viaduct having 12 arches and the SVR 22. Both were built during the 1840's, by the Shrewsbury & Birmingham Railway and the Birmingham, Wolverhampton & Stour Valley Railway companies respectively, these subsequently being absorbed, again respectively, by the Great Western and the London & North Western railways. The SVR structure was electrified during the mid 1960's but that at Oxley not until 1970, the line over it down from Wolverhampton North Junction being at that time the first of any GWR lines to be so treated. Oxley viaduct (or just beyond it) also marked the furthest point North reached by Brunel's projected Broad Gauge line from Paddington to the Mersey.

Simon Dewey

Preserved GWR "Castle" class 4-6-0 No 5043 "Earl of Mount Edgcumbe" heads North over the Stour Valley viaduct towards Bushbury on a special train to Chester from Tyseley on 22nd October 2016. The metal bridge seen through the arch spanning the canal carries the once GWR line from Stafford Road Junction to the Low Level station which prior to 1983 curved

Right beyond the canal bridge past the coaling stage of Stafford Road shed but now curves sharply round to the Left as the Bushbury Chord, connecting to the remnants of the OWWR line's northernmost extremity near Bushbury Junction, which 5043 will pass in a little over a minute.

Simon Dewey

The full length of the SVR viaduct as seen from Showell Road, looking South in the early 1970's with a Class 40-hauled express of BR Mark I carriages heading North. The floodlights of Wolves' football ground at Molineux are visible in the Left distance.

Brian Robbins

A short distance towards Bushbury from the Northern end of the viaduct the railway on its embankment passes Showell Pool off Showell Road, beyond which is seen a Southbound parcels train hauled by a Class 81 electric locomotive in 1971.

The pool was the site of the launch in 1866 of Wolverhampton's first lifeboat, appropriately named "Wolverhampton" and sent to the Swansea station, housed at Mumbles, where it served until wrecked in 1883, saving 78 lives in its career.

The tall chimneys in the background are those at Courtauld's Dunstall Hall works where their internal railway system was worked by a small number of 0-4-0 saddle tanks. For a couple of months in 1957 ex- L&YR "Pug" No 51204 stood in while Courtauld's own locomotives were temporarily out of commission.

Simon Dewey

43

Upper photo: A northbound express from Euston to the North diverted along the Grand Junction line, of BR Mark 3 stock hauled by a Class 87 electric locomotive, all in Virgin trains livery, passes the junction with the Stour Valley line at Bushbury in June 2002. The Stour Valley line curves away to the right up towards its viaduct.

A station was opened in 1852 occupying the land between and alongside the SVR and GJR lines lasting until May 1912 when it was closed, its role as a ticket collection point having ceased in 1910 and fares amounting to only £42 having been taken during 1911. No trace of the station remains today..

Lower photo: Also seen from Bushbury Lane bridge but looking North, an express hauled by Class 85 No 85 002 approaches Bushbury Junction in October 1982, passing the site, on the right, of Bushbury engine shed and on the left the remnants of Bushbury sidings, beyond which is Goodyear's tyre factory, at that time in full production. Only a Down goods loop remains of the once quite extensive sidings, their use having ceased by the late 1970's
Both: Simon Dewey

Looking Northwards again from Bushbury Lane bridge but on 6th June 2009. Only the clock tower of Goodyear's once substantial tyre factory complex remains to be seen as preserved LNER A4 No 60007 in its early BR blue livery passes Southwards returning to Banbury from Chester on a Steam Dreams "Cathedrals Express" which will take the "Old Line" towards Portobello Junction and Bescot, bypassing Wolverhampton.

Simon Dewey

Bushbury Shed

An engine shed housing about a dozen locomotives was opened at Bushbury by the LNWR in about 1860 replacing their first Wolverhampton shed opened in 1852 just North of High Level station which had become outgrown. By 1882 this shed also had become too small for its increasing allocation of locomotives and in 1883 a larger shed replaced it on the same site. This shed, brick-built with eight roads, served Wolverhampton's ex LNWR and LMS lines until the 1960's when it was closed in April 1965. Workstained Stanier Mogul 2-6-0 No 42957 together with another of the same class stand,

both in steam, at the front of the shed on 4th April 1965 only eight days before the shed's closure.

Bushbury was home to three of the class at the time, 42957 which had been transferred there from Bescot in August 1964 together with 42983 to replace two similar locomotives withdrawn during that and the previous month and 42946. All three were transferred to Oxley on closure of the shed. Seven months later Both 42957 and 42983 were subsequently moved to Heaton Mersey but 42946 was condemned at the same time.

Paul Dorney

Among the shed's allocation were a number of LMS 4F 0-6-0's and one, No 44302, is seen with others of the same class stored out of use just beyond the shed's turntable in the Spring of 1963. It was not officially withdrawn until April 1964 but is unlikely to have seen any further use however.

Simon Dewey

"Britannia" Pacific No 70050 "Firth of Clyde" then of Crewe North shed stands at Bushbury on 7th March 1964. Only 10 years old at the time, it was one of the last six of the class built, all originally allocated to the Scottish Region. Like the other five it carried the name of a Scottish Firth. It was withdrawn in August 1966.   *Bob Yate*

Bushbury's own Black 5 No 45405 stands outside the shed with 2-6-4T 42062 on 28th March 1965. Introduced in 1934 with production stretching over the next 16 years the Black 5's eventually numbered no fewer than 842 locomotives. 45405 was a relatively early member of the class, being built in 1937 by Sir W.G. Armstrong Whitworth & Co Ltd in Newcastle-upon-Tyne, one of 326 built by that firm for the LMS between 1935 and 1938. It survived until August 1967, one year before the end of BR steam operations.

Paul Dorney

While the shed's main complement was steam locomotives it did play host in its latter days to not only an allocation of Diesel shunters but also, from their introduction in the later 1950's, to Diesel multiple units from local workings as well as visiting main line Diesel locomotives. One such, English Electric Class 40 No D373, is seen on shed in the company of Black 5 and Super D locomotives in June 1963.

Simon Dewey

Wolverhampton North Junction

Wolverhampton North Junction lies about ¼ mile South of the SVR viaduct where the old S & BR line up from Oxley and Stafford Road Junction meets the SVR line leading to High Level station. A Southbound express hauled by an unidentified Class 40 Diesel is seen at the junction in September 1984. Goodyear's factory is visible in the distance above the nose of the locomotive.

The junction was first created in the 1840's when the railways in Wolverhampton were in their infancy but it was severed in the 1850's following the S&BR amalgamating with the GWR and the SVR being enveloped by the L&NWR, bitter rivals in competition over traffic to London from the Shrewsbury direction.

The junction was reinstated in 1966 in preparation for the cessation of trains for the Shrewsbury line via the Low Level route.

Simon Dewey

Looking South along the S&BR line near its bridge over Fox's Lane in April 1986.
North Junction can be just seen in the distance with a Southbound HST from the SVR line heading towards High Level station. Class 25 No 25 202 and an unidentified Class 20 running light in tandem from Oxley are held at signals awaiting clearance of the HST which they will follow towards the station.

From about this point Northwards to Stafford Road Junction the line passed through Stafford Road Works during its active existence from 1849 to 1964.

Simon Dewey

Stafford Road Junction

Stafford Road Junction lies immediately South of Oxley Viaduct on the Shrewsbury & Birmingham line where the GWR line of 1854 from Cannock Road Junction joins it. *(Below)* Looking South from adjacent to Stafford Road Junction signal box in the late 1950's a "Castle" hauling the Northbound "Cambrian Coast Express" is seen rounding the curve onto Stafford Road Junction from Dunstall Park, having left Low Level station a few minutes earlier on its journey from Paddington to Aberystwyth and Pwllheli. The locomotive will be changed at Shrewsbury with probably either a "Manor" or Standard Class 4 4-6-0 taking the train on into Wales.

Of interest is the old GWR clerestory roofed carriage in Engineer's use together with a "Toad" brake van parked on the siding that served the Horse Platform where horses were offloaded from trains visiting for race meetings at Dunstall Park racecourse.

Buildings forming the smithy and forge of Stafford Road Works form the backdrop to the picture on the right. These would be demolished some 20 years later leaving negligible evidence of the site's previous use.

F G Richardson/Ned Williams Collection

(Left) The junction looking North from adjacent to the GWR line from Dunstall Park in September 1975 with its controlling semaphore Home signals as a Class 47 on a train from Shrewsbury approaches off Oxley viaduct.

Simon Dewey

Stafford Road Works

The basis of what would become Stafford Road Works was established just South of Oxley viaduct as their locomotive shed, carriage and wagon shed, repair shop and offices by the Shrewsbury & Birmingham Railway following their reaching Wolverhampton in 1849.

It expanded over the years, in conjunction with development of the land at the lower level on the opposite side of the Stafford Road to become only second in importance to Swindon as the GWR's locomotive building and repair facility, building almost 1000 locomotives there between 1859 and 1908 as well as many rebuilds.

The physical constraints of the site ruled against its greater expansion to directly rival Swindon and the facilities by the late 1920's were outdated and unable to deal efficiently with the repair of the increased size of locomotives of the time. Accordingly in the 1930's a large modern repair shop was constructed, completed by 1932 and many of the older buildings put to new uses but new locomotive construction was not reintroduced.

The Works could thus then deal with the repair of even the largest of the GWR and subsequently BR locomotive fleet and continued so to do until the run-down of steam, the Works outshopping its last repaired locomotive, 28XX Class 2-8-0 No 2859 on 11th February 1964 and formally closing on 1st June that year.

The reception sidings for Stafford Road Works lay almost adjacent to the junction, to its West. *(Above)* In wintry conditions in about 1960 57XX Class 0-6-0 PT No 9768 stands in the reception sidings awaiting admission to the Works together with a 28XX 2-8-0 and a Large Prairie tank locomotive. Being an Oxley engine 9768 will have had only a short journey being hauled from its home shed, having already been partially stripped of various pipework before setting out. The reasons for its visit to the Works are unknown.

F G Richardson/Ned Williams Collection

Views inside the 1932-built repair shop in the late 1950's :-

(Above) 4575 Class Small Prairie 2-6-2T No 5541 approaching completion of a Heavy General repair in about 1959 with repainting well advanced. This class of engines was a later development with increased water capacity of the last type of locomotives built new at Wolverhampton , Nos. 4500 to 4519 , clearly identifiable from their predecessors by their larger tanks with sloping tops. 5541, built at Swindon in 1928 was withdrawn in July 1962 when it was purchased by Woodham Brothers in whose scrapyard at Barry it lingered for ten years before being acquired by the Dean Forest Railway who have restored it to full working order. *F G Richardson/Ned Williams Collection*

(Right) On rare occasions the works undertook repairs to other than BR's own locomotives, and NCB Austerity 0-6-0ST No 8 from Baggeridge Colliery is seen in 1960 during repair almost certainly involving tyre turning. Saddle tanks were a staple Stafford Road product for many years in the 19th Century but No 8 was a machine of a different time, being built in 1952 by the Hunslet Engine Company (works number 3776). The locomotive survives in preservation, currently bearing the name "Sir Robert Peel" and is located at the Embsay & Bolton Abbey Steam Railway in North Yorkshire.

Both: F G Richardson/Ned Williams Collection

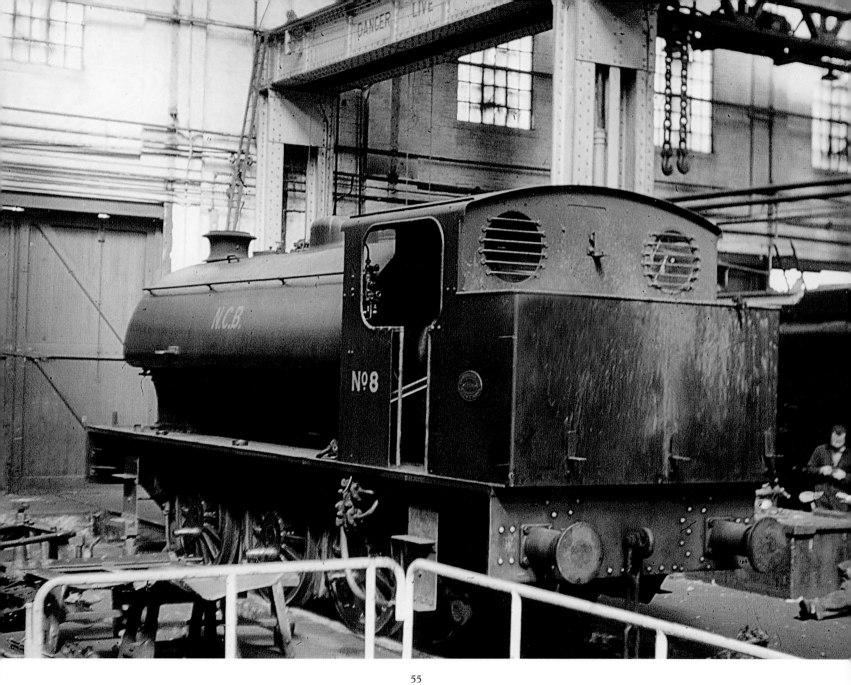

Wolverhampton (High Level) station and approaches

Lock No 3 of the 21 locks on the BCN down from Broad Street to Aldersley Junction where the BCN joins the Staffs & Worcester canal forms the foreground to a view of an unidentified Inter City 125 HST as it crosses the skew bridge spanning the canal and approaches Wolverhampton in May 2000. Although introduced in 1976, IC 125's did not commence working on services through Wolverhampton until May 1984.

While the train is in Virgin livery, the power car is in Inter City Swallow livery from which it would be repainted into Virgin's corporate colours in due course."

Simon Dewey

An unidentified Class 86 electric locomotive heads its train away from Wolverhampton station alongside the canal in July 1985. 40 of the 100 Class 86 locomotives, initially designated Class AL6 when introduced in 1965, were built by BR at Doncaster and 60 by English Electric at Vulcan Foundry as the first of BR's second generation a.c. locomotives following their experience with Classes 81 to 85.

Littles Lane bridge over the canal occupies the right of the picture with the terrace of Lock Keepers' cottages at Broad Street Basin beyond.

Simon Dewey

"Jubilee" No 45705 "Seahorse" is seen approaching High Level station from the North with a train from Blackpool where the locomotive was shedded, in about 1962. Visible in the background is the then Western Region's Herbert Street Goods Depot on the far side of the canal from the line into High Level. Following closure the building was used by a local builders' merchants but was demolished following a severe fire in 2012.

Built at Crewe in May 1936 "Seahorse" lasted until November 1965.
In the 1950's Bushbury shed was home to up to no fewer than 10 "Jubilees" for the Wolverhampton –Birmingham- London (Euston) services which were transferred away when these were reduced preparatory to WCML electrification and the services to London (Paddington) from Low Level increased to suit.

John Bucknall

LMS "Jinty" 0-6-0T No 47473 of Bushbury shed acting as station pilot on 28th February 1959 propels empty coaching stock out of the station towards the carriage shed which existed a couple of hundred yards North of the bridge over Wednesfield Road. It is passing Wolverhampton No 3 Signal Box, one of four controlling lines in and beyond each end of the station until rebuilding of the station in the mid 1960's and construction of the

Wolverhampton Power box opened when the line was electrified.
The "Jinties", introduced in 1924 were the standard shunting engines of the LMS, based upon an earlier Midland Railway design and totalling no fewer than 422 in number. 47473 emerged new from the Vulcan Foundry in December 1927 and lasted until 1962, being withdrawn from Bushbury shed.

Alan Davies Collection

The station seen from the North in 1986 ...

A Class 47 locomotive stands on one of the lines adjacent to the Down bay platform (then designated Platform 4 but now Platform 6) awaiting the arrival of an electric-hauled express from Euston which it will take on to Shrewsbury, while another 47 with an electric locomotive in tow has arrived with a train at Platform 1 (the main Down platform). Over to the far left stands a Class 86 electric locomotive stabled on one of the lines that would disappear a few years later when an additional platform (the current Platform 4) was built.

....and in 2017

Together with the new Platform 4 a new footbridge was built in 2004 towards the Northern end of the station and the island platform (Platforms 2 and 3) extended to accommodate longer trains. The new footbridge dominates the 2017 photograph as A1 Class Pacific No 60136 "Tornado" prepares to leave from Platform 1 with the "Border Raider" steam-hauled special train to Carlisle on 16th September. "Tornado" was built, appropriately for an LNER designed locomotive, at Darlington and completed in 2008 being the first brand new British main line steam locomotive built since "Evening Star" in 1960.

The station is earmarked for radical rebuilding as part of the Wolverhampton Interchange Project , initial works on which had commenced by the time of writing. *Both: Simon Dewey*

The High Level station was opened in 1852 as Wolverhampton General station jointly serving the London & North Western and Shrewsbury & Birmingham railway companies. Its name changed to Wolverhampton Queen Street in 1853 and to Wolverhampton High Level in 1885. Use by S&BR trains ceased after that company amalgamated with the GWR and began to use the Low Level station from 1854.

A 220 yard long drive ran from the end of Queen Street, at the time Wolverhampton's principal thoroughfare, to the station, at the Queen Street end of which was the arched entrance building seen in the photograph. As built, the entrances, the two larger ones for carriages and the smaller ones each side for pedestrians, possessed wrought iron gates but these were subsequently removed and the openings bricked up.

The upper storey of the building contained offices and the S&BR's Board Room. In later years the building was used as offices by the LNWR's and its descendents' Goods Department. The 3 storey buildings each side were demolished in the 1970's but the building itself remains, being Listed Grade 2. It is known now as the Queens Building and accommodates a coffee house in the ground storey.

Michael Hale / Ned Williams collection

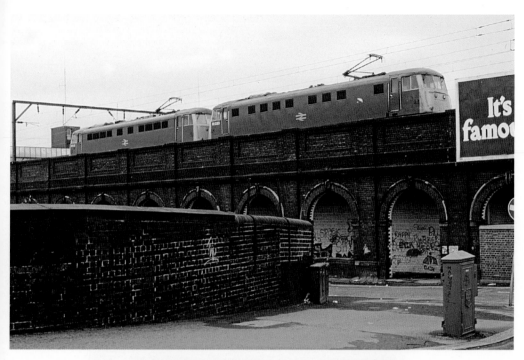

Before the new Platform 4 was built the lines that prior to 1967 had formed the goods avoiding lines and sidings were used for stabling locomotives between duties. Two electric locomotives, 81 020 and an unidentified Class 85 stand in 1986 on one of the lines above the arcade created when the original station was enlarged in the 1880's. The arcade extends from Wednesfield Road to give access at its southern end to the Low Level station forecourt with a subway joining it about midway along via steps down from the High Level station forecourt and until the mid-1960's from the Up platform of the station also.

All: Simon Dewey

Two unidentified Class 87 locomotives stand with their trains at the Northern end of the station in July 1988, both having arrived from the South, that on the left in its standard blue livery being a train from Euston terminating at Wolverhampton but that on the right, in its more colourful Inter-City livery, proceeding North.

Following the introduction of DVT's later that year the Euston train would return Southwards with the locomotive, now at the rear, propelling the train. At the time of the photograph however it would proceed to Oxley carriage sidings where it would run round its train before towing it back to the station for its return working.

Curving round at the right of the picture is the then Platform 4 from which, at the time, trains starting from Wolverhampton left for Shrewsbury and the Cambrian Coast before these services were extended to Birmingham.

Simon Dewey

Unique Network Rail Class 950 Test unit No 950 001 is set to leave Platform 4 on 26th July 2009. The unit, based upon a Class 150/1 "Sprinter" bodyshell and constructed by BR at York in 1987, is a purpose-built 2-car Diesel multiple unit formed of two driving motor vehicles, Nos DM990600 and 990601. Operating from Derby RTC it is equipped with video cameras and other recording equipment to carry out track assessment duties usually on lines where locomotive-hauled trains are not allowed. The circumstances of its visit to Wolverhampton were not discovered. *Simon Dewey*

At the Southern end of the station in 1980 a Class 86 electric enters Platform 1 with a train from Euston while on the extreme left another of the class No 86 235 " Novelty " in its Rainhill 150 livery, can just be seen awaiting departure with an express to Euston.

On the extreme right can be seen the nose of Class 40, No 40 055 waiting in the bay platform which at the time served the Parcels depot of the station.
The buildings in the background are those of Mill Street Goods Depot.

Simon Dewey

By 2009 the old order has changed, with Euston trains now being formed of Virgin "Pendolino" units, one of which is seen awaiting departure from Platform 3.

Locomotive haulage of passenger trains through Wolverhampton was by this time a rarity apart from the short-lived Wrexham & Shropshire company's trains running to Marylebone, of which there were initially 5 each way per day but subsequently reduced to 4 and ultimately to 3.

The service only ran from April 2008 to January 2011, its lack of profitability and early cessation in part being due to London-bound passengers not being permitted to board at Wolverhampton nor to alight on their return.

Trains were formed using a DB Schenker Class 67 locomotive, Ex BR Mark 3 coaches and a DVT, although initially trains were topped and tailed by 67's.

67 010 in its distinctive grey and silver livery is seen at Platform 2 with a Southbound W&S train. The middle line has been removed from between Platforms 1 and 2 and in the background, on the site of the Low Level line beyond Wednesfield Road bridge, students' residential blocks have been built.

Simon Dewey

For a period in the 1980's services from Paddington to Wolverhampton were revived although traversing the West Midlands via Coventry and Birmingham New Street. The trains were often in the hands of Class 50 locomotives, their principal activities on the Western Region having been taken over by HST's releasing them for other duties.

50 027 "Lion" enters Wolverhampton station on a train from Paddington in July 1986. The locomotive was built at Vulcan Foundry in 1968, entering traffic in the June of that year. Like the rest of the class its early years were spent on the then unelectrified WCML between Crewe and Glasgow. When the route was electrified the class was transferred to the Western Region and worked on trains from Paddington to the West Country as well as, later, SR Waterloo to Exeter services. Withdrawn in July 1991 50 027 was not scrapped and is preserved on the Mid Hants Railway.

Simon Dewey

A view from the roof of the current station car park looking South in 1986. A Class 47 awaits departure from Platform 3 with a southbound train while a train from Euston hauled by a Class 86 electric enters platform 1. Beyond the 47 is the then Wolverhampton power signal box commissioned when the line was electrified in 1967 with, beyond that, Sun Street bridge at the southern end of what was Low Level station. To the immediate right is J.N.Miller's flour and provender mill, now demolished and beyond that the buildings of the LNWR's Mill Street Goods depot.

The line round towards Heath Town Junction curves away to the left from Crane Street Junction which the rear coaches of the arriving train are just crossing. In the middle distance is the Osier Beds steelworks which at that time possessed its own small fleet of Diesel shunting engines. The line closest to the photographer forms the South Bay, Platform 5, used by local trains from Birmingham New Street terminating at Wolverhampton.   *Simon Dewey*

Crane Street Junction lies just South of Wolverhampton station where the line to Heath Town Junction and Portobello leaves the Stour Valley route to Birmingham via Dudley Port. On Summer Saturdays in the 1980's and 90's locomotive-hauled trains ran from Birmingham to Pwllheli on the Cambrian Coast, often double headed, initially by pairs of Class 25's but later by 31's and ultimately 37's.

Such a train is seen rounding the SVR onto Crane Street Junction in August 1983 hauled by an unidentified pair of Class 25's.

Simon Dewey

The line from Crane Street Junction to Heath Town Junction was built by the nominally independent Wolverhampton & Walsall Railway in 1872 but purchased initially by the LNWR who soon sold it on to the Midland Railway although the line was worked jointly by both companies. Beyond Heath Town the line extended across Wednesfield Heath and on to Ryecroft Junction at Walsall.

In 1881 a link line was constructed by the LNWR from Heath Town down to Portobello Junction near Willenhall where it connects to the GJR route between Bushbury and Bescot. The line on towards Walsall from Heath Town was severed as a through route when the M6 motorway was built and subsequently cut back in stages first to Willenhall then to Wednesfield where it remained worked as a siding until final closure in 1983.

A special Orient Express working returning from Chester hauled by Class 33 No 33 027 "Earl Mountbatten of Burma" is seen between Crane Street and Heath Town Junctions after passing the Osier Beds steel works in July 1984. In the Right foreground is the link down from Heath Town Junction to the Low Level station.

The appearance of a Class 33 in the town was unusual but not unprecedented.

Simon Dewey

Wednesfield Road Goods Depot and Heath Town Junction

The line to Heath Town Junction runs on the embankment in the background as Class 47 No 47 350 which has become derailed in Wednesfield Road Goods Depot receives the attention of the Bescot breakdown train in April 1985. The large number of Presflo cement wagons present in the Depot yard arose from their being stored there pending removal for scrapping. Access into the Depot was gained down from Heath Town Junction and in steam days trains departing up to the junction frequently required assistance from the depot shunter, itself more often than not an ex LMS tender engine.

The 47/3 subclass of locomotives were originally built without any train heating equipment and remained almost exclusively freight locomotives all their working lives.

Simon Dewey

The depot was opened by the Midland Railway in 1881 and to the end of its days bore the wording "Midland Railway Goods and Grain Warehouse" on the projecting brickwork band at first floor level across its southern elevation. It was a busy depot until the mid 1960's when West Midland goods activity became centred on the then newly-remodelled Bescot Yard although use of Wednsfield Road continued until the late 1980's when it became part of Wolverhampton Steel Terminal. As the economic climate changed its use reduced and the depot was closed and subsequently demolished, despite having Grade 2 Listed Building status, in the 1990's. A large Royal Mail sorting office now occupies the site, with a crane salvaged from the building outside serving as a memento of its past use.

Simon Dewey

Right up to the final day of regular steam operations in Wolverhampton Wednesfield Road Goods Depot received visits from steam locomotives. Stanier 8F 2-8-0 No 48674 departs from the depot and begins its climb up to Heath Town Junction with probably the last steam-hauled train from the yard on Friday 4th March 1967.

48674 was one of the wartime 8F's built at the Southern Railway's works at Ashford in Kent in March 1944. It survived until within 9 months of the end of BR steam, being withdrawn in November 1967.

Roger Fletcher

A view of Heath Town Junction in the mid 1980's. A Class 81-hauled express approaches on the LNWR 1881 link line up from Portobello Junction while a pair of Class 20's stand on the remnants of the Midland Railway line to Walsall, lifted by this time beyond Deans Road about ¼ mile away. The 20's had pulled out of Wednesfield Road Goods and will await clearance forwards onto the line into High Level after the passenger train has passed. The sharpness of the curve round from the summit of the line rising from Portobello can be gauged by the end of the passenger train whose last carriage is visible in the distance.

Simon Dewey

Low Level to Cannock Road

Black 5 No 44865 had the distinction of being the locomotive of the last regular steam-hauled passenger train from Wolverhampton on Friday March 3rd 1967 when it took forward the 15.10 Paddington to Birkenhead express that had arrived at Low Level behind a Brush Class 47 Diesel . In the failing light of the rather cold, grey, late afternoon 44865, wearing a wreath on its smokebox door, departs vigorously past the station's North signal box with its train of BR Mark 1 stock.

The following two days marked the end of through services from Paddington to Birkenhead celebrated by two steam hauled specials on each day, "Castles" Nos 7029 "Clun Castle" and 4079 "Pendennis Castle" on the Saturday and 7029 again and Black 5 No 44680 on the Sunday.

The newly-electrified services from High Level station to Euston commenced on Monday 6th March. Sunday 5th March 1967 also saw the end of trolleybus operation in Wolverhampton. Both the Black 5's involved lasted only a further 6 months, both being withdrawn in the September. Both "Castles" remain in preservation however.

David Rostance

The GWR's main Wolverhampton carriage sidings were located at Cannock Road. Here the bulk of them lay adjacent to and encompassed the OWWR line between Cannock Road and Bushbury Junctions with a total of eight lines variously capable of storing between 14 and 17 65-feet coaches. Following the introduction of Diesel multiple units on local services in the later 1950's two of the sidings were equipped to service these units.

The prestige Birmingham Pullman train was introduced in 1960 and was based at Cannock Road, making a return trip from Low Level to Paddington each weekday with a fill-in return Paddington to Birmingham working between. It is seen here shortly after its introduction in its Nanking Blue livery with white windows and the Pullman Car Company crest on the front and sides. In many ways it and its sister trains the Midland Pullman and Bristol Pullman were the forerunners of the Inter City 125 HST's introduced in 1976 and still in operation. The Birmingham Pullman ceased to run after 3rd March 1967 on the cessation of through working from Low Level to Paddington.

F G Richardson/Ned Williams Collection

From the 1970's until the power station's closure in 2015, Merry-Go-Round trains serving Ironbridge Power Station with coal from collieries North of Wolverhampton traversed the remnants of the OWWR line between Bushbury and Cannock Road Junctions thence the GWR line round to Stafford Road Junction to join the Shrewsbury & Birmingham route to head back Northwards. Loaded trains travelled up the line fully to Cannock Road Junction where they required to reverse, the locomotive uncoupling, running round its train and pushing it clear of Cannock Road to then return towing it forwards to continue its journey.

Empty trains did the same in reverse.

While interesting to watch, this manoeuvre was decidedly inconvenient so in 1983 a new length of railway was opened, the Bushbury Chord, sharply curving round between the GWR line east of Dunstall Park and reconnecting to the OWWR line South of Bushbury Junction, obviating the need for the operations at Cannock Road, the lines to which were lifted. Class 47 No 47 214 on a returning empty MGR train has arrived at Cannock Road in the late 1970's from Ironbridge ready to commence its reversal manoeuvres.   *Simon Dewey*

Above: Class 47 No D1823 in weathered two tone green livery heads a loaded MGR train off the GJR line (the "Old Line") at Bushbury Junction round onto the OWWR line towards Cannock Road in 1971.

Right: At about this point a Limit of Shunt board adjacent to the left-hand track marked the boundary between the lines controlled by BR's Western Region and its London Midland Region. On 1st January 1963 this demarcation ceased to exist with the transfer of all the WR's lines and installations in the West Midlands to the London Midland Region. *Both: Simon Dewey*

The "Old Line" as it leaves Bushbury towards Bescot flanks the North Eastern edge of Fowler's Park Playing Fields at Park Village before crossing the Cannock Road. A footpath leading to Park Lane from the playing fields crosses the railway on the level while another from Prosser Street, Park Village crossed by way of the footbridge seen to the Right of the photograph.

(left) The spire of Heath Town church is visible in the background as Caprotti valve geared BR Standard Class 5 4-6-0 No 73131 heads tender first with a train of empty cattle wagons Southwards in April 1963.

Erection of catenary for electrification of the line had not yet commenced but preparatory works including replacing the old footbridge with a new, loftier one to accommodate the overhead wires were advancing. This section of line, once wiring was completed, was the first in Wolverhampton to be energised, in January 1966 but not used until two months later.

Simon Dewey

Approaching the foot crossing referred to in the previous photograph but some 40 years later preserved LMS "Coronation" Pacific No 6233 "Duchess of Sutherland" passes Southwards beneath the wires with a VSOE Northern Belle train heading towards Bescot and Walsall on 25th April 2003.

The chimney of Goodyear's tyre factory is visible in the distance and the buildings the train is passing are part of the Wolverhampton Cold Store off Park Lane.

Simon Dewey

As the "Old Line" heads through Park Village it enters a cutting and passes through the 200 yard long Wolverhampton Tunnel a little way South of the site of the first Wolverhampton station, the GJR's Wednesfield Heath station of 1837. All traces of the station are now gone but the buildings remained in existence until after electrification of the line in the late 1960's. The GJR merged with the London & Birmingham Railway in 1846 to form the London & North Western railway, the country's first trunk route.

While now usually used mainly by freight trains the "Old Line" acts as a diversionary route when engineering works on the West Coast Main line between Rugby and Stafford are taking place and passenger trains can again be seen.

One such diverted Euston to Glasgow express hauled by an unidentified Class 87 is seen after leaving the tunnel in October 1981.

It is interesting to note that the original name of the road running parallel to the railway at this point was Station Road until the late 1990's.

Simon Dewey

Portobello Junction

About a mile South of the tunnel at Wednesfield Heath lies Portobello Junction where the LNWR's 1881-built link line from Heath Town Junction meets the GJR. The unique BR Class 8 Pacific No 71000 "Duke of Gloucester" heads North along the "Old Line" with a commemorative special train in April 1996 with Diesel back-up in the form of an RES-liveried Class 47 marshalled behind the steam locomotive. The line to Heath Town Junction is seen leaving to the Right.

A view of Portobello Junction looking North with an express approaching on the LNWR link from Heath Town Junction in the late 1980's. The "Old Line" is that heading away on the Right.

It was here on the morning of October 19th 1899 that a passenger train on the line down from Heath Town ran into an also Southbound goods train proceeding along the "Old Line" but which in thick fog had passed signals at danger giving precedence to the passenger train onto the junction. The crew of the passenger train's locomotive, both Bushbury men, were killed. Their derailed and damaged locomotive, a Ramsbottom "DX" Class 0-6-0 No 278, however was subsequently repaired and survived until 1919.

Both: Simon Dewey

The Stour Valley line South of High Level and Monmore Green

A Class 47-hauled train departs from Wolverhampton station on a cold day in February 1986, approaching Crane Street Junction from where it will take the Stour Valley route through the Black Country towards Birmingham via Coseley, Tipton and Dudley Port.

The taller buildings in the background were those of J.N.Miller's flour and provender mill, now demolished. That on the immediate left is the end of one of the LNWR Mill Street Goods depot buildings.

Simon Dewey

The LMS and GWR lines to the High and Low Level stations respectively ran almost parallel to each other as they approached their station from the South but as the station names indicate, at distinctly different levels. The LMS line (the Stour Valley line) runs predominantly on embankment or viaduct with the GWR line in a cutting until it entered a tunnel starting below Lower Horseley Fields and emerging almost at Low Level station itself. The disparity in levels of the two lines can be clearly seen in this view towards the Southern end of Low Level tunnel from Lower Walsall Street bridge where it crosses the old GWR trackbed.
A Class 86- hauled Euston express heads South at elevated level as it leaves the town in the early 1980's.

Simon Dewey

About ¼ mile South of the previous picture the SVR passes Chillington Fields, off the Bilston Road, where is the LNWR's canal transhipment shed, now part of Wolverhampton Steel Terminal. Here a short arm off the BCN canal terminates in a basin within the structure, with raised platforms each side flanked by railway tracks. Goods could thus be readily transferred between canal barges and railway wagons for onward shipment either by canal or railway.

Rail access is via a branch off the SVR at Monmore Green which also serves the current Steel Terminal complex developed on the site of the previous Walsall |Street goods depot of the Oxford Worcester & Wolverhampton Railway. Until the early years of the present century it also served the adjacent British Oxygen works but such use has now ceased.

Simon Dewey

Class 25's Nos 25 145 and 25 162 stand on the branch off the SVR serving the steel terminal and British Oxygen works double heading a train of empty liquid oxygen tank wagons from the latter awaiting departure up to the SVR line in October 1983. Delivery of loaded tank wagons and removal of empty ones took place on a daily basis, the empty train leaving during the afternoon to join the SVR and travel South to Soho Junction, thence to Perry Barr to join the GJR and return Northwards repassing Wolverhampton some half an hour or more after leaving. Workings to the British Oxygen works have now ceased but the branch remains in use serving the steel terminal.

Simon Dewey

English Electric Class 40 No 40 076 stands on the bridge over Bilston Road at Monmore Green of the spur into Wolverhampton Steel Terminal just short of its junction with the SVR on 3rd May 1982. 40 076 was, like the two 25's in the previous photograph, about to collect empty liquid oxygen tanks for train 6F57. A WMPTE MCW/Daimler Fleetline bus No 6795 approaches on a Route 79 Birmingham-Wolverhampton via West Bromwich working. The Midland Metro tramway now passes along the road. *David Rostance*

Wolverhampton's most recent railway is the Midland Metro opened in 1999 running from the city to Birmingham, for much of the route using that of the old GWR line to Birmingham Snow Hill. Coming from Birmingham on the GWR route it leaves this at Stow Heath to run at street level along Bilston Road into the city centre terminating at the time of writing at St George's Parade but in the process of being extended to Wolverhampton railway station.

At the same location as the previous photograph but in October 1999 shortly after the commencement of services, tram No 14 is seen heading out from Wolverhampton along Bilston Road approaching the bridges carrying the Stour Valley line and beyond that the spur to Wolverhampton Steel terminal. No 14 was one of the original fleet of 16 Type T69 trams with which the Metro opened but that fleet was replaced by newer Urbos 3 vehicles between 2014 and 2016.   *Simon Dewey*

During the Metro's construction use was made of contractors' locomotives such as Grant Rail Ruston Hornsby 0-4-0 Diesel shunter No 5, seen on 24th July 1998 with a short train of ballast wagons near Priestfield where the tramway emerges onto Bilston Road.

Roger Fletcher